Voyager

A play

Tony Rushforth

Samuel French — London
www.samuelfrench-london.co.uk

ISBN 978 0 573 12294 1

VOYAGER

First performed on 4 November 2011 at the Questors Theatre, Ealing, with the following cast:

Isabel	Anne Neville
Margot	Caroline Bleakley
Stephen	Lewis Brown
Waiter	Tony Barber

Directed by Tony Rushforth
Designed by Bron Blake

PRODUCTION NOTES

It is important that the carefully plotted costume changes and the minimal property and furniture changes between scenes are handled very swiftly so as not to affect the play's overall momentum. In the original production such scenes were executed by Mario with another waiter dressed in a matching waiter's costume.

The play should open with the plotted music as detailed for the ending of the play, i.e. a vibrant short sequence from Mozart's *Piano Concerto No. 23*.

The appropriate, atmospheric music for the changes between scenes might draw from the repertoire of a "Palm Court Orchestra" similar to the one mentioned in the text.

ERRATUM

In the first performance of *Voyager* Stephen was played by Tony Barber and the Waiter by Lewis Brown, not the other way round as listed above.

COPYRIGHT INFORMATION
(See also page ii)

This play is fully protected under the Copyright Laws of the British Commonwealth of Nations, the United States of America and all countries of the Berne and Universal Copyright Conventions.

All rights, including Stage, Motion Picture, Radio, Television, Public Reading, and Translation into Foreign Languages, are strictly reserved.

No part of this publication may lawfully be reproduced in ANY form or by any means — photocopying, typescript, recording (including video-recording), manuscript, electronic, mechanical, or otherwise — or be transmitted or stored in a retrieval system, without prior permission.

Licences are issued subject to the understanding that it shall be made clear in all advertising matter that the audience will witness an amateur performance; that the names of the authors of the plays shall be included on all announcements and on all programmes; and that the integrity of the authors' work will be preserved.

The Royalty Fee is subject to contract and subject to variation at the sole discretion of Samuel French Ltd.

In Theatres or Halls seating Four Hundred or more the fee will be subject to negotiation.

In Territories Overseas the fee quoted in this Acting Edition may not apply. A fee will be quoted on application to our local authorized agent, or if there is no such agent, on application to Samuel French Ltd, London.

CHARACTERS

Isabel, 70
Margot, her daughter, 44
Stephen, 70
Waiter, Mario, early/ mid-20s

The action of the play takes place on the deck of a cruise liner sailing on the Baltic Sea

Time — the present

SYNOPSIS OF SCENES

For Jack and James

VOYAGER

Scene 1

A section of the deck of a cruise ship. Mid afternoon — it is warm and sunny

We can see at least part of an expansive sky which changes according to the time and the weather. The setting is "representational" rather than totally realistic. There are white ship's railings across about half of the upstage plane with some set L at an angle. Some suggestion of the ship's floor decking could, perhaps be shown by a raised level, UR, which leads to the entrances and exits for the café/bar and cabins. UL there are two wooden, latticed chairs with arms by the side of a matching circular table and UR there is a wooden, high-backed chair with cushions and by its side is a low, latticed coffee table. UL, by the ship's railings is an isolated chair without arms. Depending on sight lines it would be very advantageous to have a section of two matching rail units which look directly out to sea (about a metre in width) and are set extreme DL and DR which from time to time could be used for Isabel's and Stephen's soliloquies. Downstage extreme R is another matching wooden latticed table, with two matching chairs without arms. There is DL an entrance/exit which goes to a lower deck

Isabel, Margot's mother, is sitting in the upright, large chair and is working on her embroidery. She is 70 years old and is trying hard not to show her age. She is attractive — she hasn't "given up". She is wearing sunglasses, a colourful buttoned dress, a

*sun hat and fashionable sandals. Her hair is discreetly dyed
and it is evident that she uses make-up. By her side on the coffee
table is her handbag and sewing bag. Margot, her daughter, is
44 and is sitting to the left of the upstage table. She is wearing
a summer skirt and a nondescript short-sleeved top, her hair
is casually tied back and she is barefoot, her flip-flops by the
side of the chair. She wears spectacles and no make-up and is
reading a travel book*

*Margot stops reading, sees her mother is preoccupied with her
embroidery, sighs, rises and paces over to the ship's rail* DL *where
the lights close in around her*

Margot I shouldn't have agreed to it. "Cruise round the Baltic
— outside cabin — sunshine — wonderful seascapes." The
brochure made it sound very attractive, very tempting; it's
Mother's idea of heaven, not mine. It's a floating hotel ... with
aspirations to be four star ... and she is quickly discovering
that it's really three star. In any case I don't want to be with
her all the time ... and we have to share a cabin which is quite
a strain ... hence I ... I find excuses to slip away — to be on
my own. (*Beat*) Of course she's canny, she knew the ports of
call would appeal ... it was blackmail and I succumbed. So ...
that's why I'm here and after only four days I feel like ... (*she
smiles*) ... like a fish out of water!
Isabel (*calling out*) Margot!

The lighting returns to its previous coverage of the full setting

(*Louder*) Margot!

Margot turns

Don't get sunburnt, it's quite strong. I have some cream,
darling ... (*She opens her bag for the cream and holds it out
towards Margot. Calling, with a somewhat commanding tone*)
Margot!

Margot crosses to her side and takes the cream, moves to the table and puts down her book

It's amazing to be so warm — and we're so far north. They were swimming in the outdoor pool — I could see when I booked to have my hair done.

Margot I was tempted ... but just too many people. (*She applies the sun cream*)

Isabel Not so rough, Margot — we don't want to encourage those little facial lines, and especially round the eyes, now do we? It must have been your long walk. I told you not to. It says on the notice: six times round and it's a mile.

Margot I did three.

Isabel Three?

Margot Miles.

Isabel That's too far — and in this heat.

Margot It passes the time. I just don't like the days at sea, the *long* days at sea.

Isabel You enjoy reading. Always your nose in a book.

Margot I can read at home.

Isabel Just relax — one needs to after the excursions. Tallinn was just too long.

Margot Well it was optional.

Isabel I didn't want you to go on your own. At least Copenhagen was all on the level. But Tallinn ... that steep climb, and for what? Those awful cobblestones.

Margot I thought it had lots of character ... most of it medieval — well, certainly the cathedral. (*She hands back the cream*) You should have worn sensible shoes. (*She sits in the upstage deck chair and reads her travel book*)

The lighting loses its warmth

Isabel They were sensible — just a small heel (*she smiles*) and rather becoming. (*She looks up to the sky*) The sun's gone in. (*She takes off her sun hat and sunglasses and looks in the direction of the off stage café*) And where is that man with the tea? (*She briefly returns to her embroidery*) I've been thinking, Margot — it does seem an unnecessary expense ... the upkeep of our separate flats. It would be far more sensible to combine — my flat's much bigger and there would be room for all your books — I could put up new shelves. Margot? Margot.

Margot looks up from her book

You're not listening.

Margot I heard. You've mentioned it before. I don't want to move. I like my independence — what little I have.

Isabel That's not a very nice thing to say.

Margot Sorry — we can talk about it later. I'm trying to work my way through the gallery for tomorrow — we'll have to be very selective, it's huge.

Isabel The gallery?

Margot Mother ... The Hermitage — *the* art gallery in St Petersburg.

The Waiter enters swiftly with tray containing teapot, milk, sugar and two cups etc. and sets them on the upstage table. He is in his early/mid twenties, handsome and charismatic and he speaks with an Italian accent. He wears his daytime clothes; black trousers and waistcoat and tie with a white shirt

Waiter Tea, *signora*.

Isabel (*rising*) You've taken a — long — time.

Waiter We are busy ... always when day at sea.

Isabel (*crossing to the table*) And the sandwiches?

Waiter Sorry, madam. Everyone having tea at same time. What do they call it? The tea in the afternoon.

Margot (*smiling*) Not quite — "the afternoon tea."

Waiter Ah yes. "The afternoon tea."

Margot An English eccentricity.

Waiter *Si*. But not only in England I think?

Margot smiles and then Isabel quickly interrupts

Isabel When you've quite finished your little *tête-a-tête*. (*To the Waiter*) My sandwiches.

Waiter (*to Isabel*) *Si signora — subito.*

The Waiter exits quickly

Isabel "*Subito*" indeed. (*She lifts up the lid of the teapot*) One teabag ... and no hot water — really. (*She starts to pour the tea*) Tea, Margot?

Margot No thanks. It's embarrassing.

Isabel What?

Margot Talking to the staff like that.

Isabel (*pointedly*) One has to preserve a certain distance, otherwise they ... they take advantage.

Margot I don't think with over two thousand passengers they have time to "take advantage." No, Mother, you like to make complaints.

Isabel Justifiable complaints. This trip is costing a lot of money.

Margot Cousin Adele's money.

Isabel Yes, poor Adele. I'm very grateful to her — and so should you be. It was a generous legacy — journey of a lifetime.

Stephen enters, walking purposefully from one side of the deck. He is a distinguished 70-year-old man, has a trim figure and is wearing light slacks, a colourful but tasteful shirt, a cravat just showing and a panama hat

Isabel smiles at him

Stephen Excuse me.

Isabel Good-afternoon.

Stephen (*taking off his hat as he crosses on his walk*) Good-afternoon.

Isabel Lovely day.

Stephen (*stopping at Isabel's words*) Yes ... yes it is.

Isabel Did I see you in Tallinn?

Stephen Yes. Remarkable, wasn't it?

Isabel Yes ... remarkable.

Stephen Did you get as far as the cathedral?

Isabel Not to be missed — medieval.

Stephen Yes. Quite special.

Isabel Oh yes.

Margot It's a pity that the long walk to the square was so com-
mercial. Just lots of tourist trash.

Stephen I suppose they're desperate for the trade.

Margot I'm sure they are.

Isabel But the market itself was fascinating.

Stephen Yes ... yes it was. (*Pause. He looks at Margot and then
back to Isabel*) Well, I must get on. (*He smiles*) Promised myself
that I would at least manage a mile. I've been lazy. This is my
first walk ... on the ship.

Margot It's easier on the promenade deck.

Stephen Is it?

Margot Yes, not so many deckchairs or tables ... more space
to walk.

Stephen Thank you. I'd prefer that.

Margot It's three decks below this. (*Pointing*) Go back down,
then take the lift — deck seven.

Stephen Thank you. (*to Isabel*) Goodbye. (*Pause*) See you at
dinner. (*He puts on his hat*)

Isabel Yes ... goodbye. (*She rises. Calling*) Enjoy your walk.

Stephen (*calling back*) I will.

Stephen exits

Isabel watches him go and rises

Isabel Quite a gentleman. You can tell. And nicely spoken
— educated. I like the panama hat. Artistic perhaps? (*Quite
strongly*) Damn it — we didn't introduce ourselves. Seeing
him. It was such a surprise.

Margot He was "passing by", no need for formalities.

Isabel These things matter — well, to my generation anyway. (*Beat*) He's on his own.

Margot How do you know?

Isabel (*sitting back at the table*) Has a table to our right, near those palms, by the double doors. (*Beat*) Not many people opt to sit on their own.

Margot Well, we did.

Isabel You mean you did. It was a mistake — I shouldn't have agreed. A "selective" table for eight would have been lovely. I'm a very sociable person and it's nice to ... to mix with others at dinner and ... and share one's experiences.

Margot Experiences?

Isabel Of life. (*She looks in the direction of Stephen's exit*) Oh yes ... he's definitely on his own. Must have been generous with the head waiter.

Margot looks at her

To get a table to himself. (*Beat*) Obviously likes to keep his own counsel.

Margot (*pointedly*) Yes. Doesn't like to socialize.

Isabel (*ignoring this*) "See you at dinner". That was charming — don't you think?

Margot Just being polite.

Isabel I noticed him looking.

Margot looks at her

At dinner ... last night. (*She smiles again*) Discreetly of course ... you have your back to him. Yes, he's in my line of vision, very much so. (*Beat*) It is formal dress tonight?

Margot No, Mother — "smart-casual".

Isabel A pity — I think it's very civilized — dressing formally for dinner.

Margot I can't stand the pretentiousness. The other night a man was turned away — by the head waiter — and all because he wasn't wearing a bow tie — ridiculous.

Isabel There's nothing quite like a man in full evening dress, Margot — rules are rules. Standards have to be maintained.

Margot Standards! This isn't a nineteen-thirties luxury cruise. I don't think Noël Coward would be impressed — when dinner is "formal" most of the dresses look as if they've come out of *Strictly Come Dancing*.

Isabel Don't be so cynical — a certain ... "opulence" doesn't do any harm.

Margot "Opulence"? Vulgar and brash.

Isabel Well you certainly can't accuse me of being vulgar.

Margot (*rising with her book and putting on her flip flops*) I'm off to the library — must do some more homework on St Petersburg.

Isabel Well, don't be long. Palm Court Orchestra at five.

Margot takes a sip of the tea which is now cold

The Waiter enters carrying a tray with a small plate of postage-stamp sandwiches, small plate, napkin and places them on the small table

Margot I'll think about it. (*She goes to leave, calling back to Isabel*) Might have a swim.

Margot exits

Isabel (*calling back*) They said the water's too cold.
Waiter Sandwiches, madam.
Isabel Lovely. (*She takes a sandwich*)
Waiter (*handing her the bill and biro*) Madam please sign?

Isabel signs the slip and Waiter gives her the copy

Waiter Sorry about delay — about mistake.
Isabel We can all make mistake — mistakes — can't we? However the tea's gone cold. Could you get me a fresh, hot brew?
Waiter Brew?

Isabel You *brew* the tea ...

The Waiter doesn't understand

　You *mash* it ...

He still doesn't understand

　... to make it ... *afresh*.

The Waiter is confused

　Oh, never mind just get me (*louder*) another — *hot pot of tea*.
Waiter Of course, madam. (*He picks up the teapot and looks where Margot made her exit*) And the nice lady? Tea later?
Isabel No. The "nice lady" has gone for a swim.
Waiter For a swim. (*He smiles*) Athletic — no?
Isabel Yes. That will be all.
Waiter (*with slight irony*) I hope you will enjoy dinner, madam.

　The Waiter gives a slight bow and exits

Isabel (*smiling*) Yes ... dinner. (*Beat*) I think I'll wear my lavender — understated yet stylish — discreet. (*She rises and looks in the direction of Stephen's exit*) Yes, the lavender will do very nicely ... (*she looks out to sea and smiles*) ... with my pearls.

The Lights fade quickly to black-out

　Isabel exits

　Margot enters

An enclosed area of light comes up on Margot by the DR rail. She is barefoot and wearing a white towelling dressing gown

Margot I'll be in trouble — I didn't go to the concert — saw
the programme: Lehar, Ivor Novello, and the dreadful soprano
we heard on the first night — "gathering lilacs". I went for a
swim ... no one else in the pool ... lovely. (*She looks around*) I
like it at this time. Quiet. The restaurant all ready, the waiters
having a sneaky cigarette before "curtain up", before the
hurly burly. And the guests? All changing for dinner ... totally
preoccupied with the ritual — especially the women. (*Beat*)
Mother will be in the midst of all her preparations. But tonight
she has additional motivation — I know the signals. Her focus
is now on the "man of mystery", alone at his separate table,
yet in her line of vision. O, charming man in panama hat, take
care — Mother's beady eye is on you.

Margot exits

Stephen enters

The light cross fades to Stephen in the DL *rail area enclosed in
light. He is wearing a lightweight suit, conventional shirt and a
subdued tie. He carries a glass of gin and tonic*

Stephen I don't go into dinner straight away — when the doors
open, so to speak. In any case there's no delay ordering the
menu as that has to be decided the night before — rather like
being in hospital — if you ever have? But the food is better ...
than the hospital. (*Beat*) Once the pianist has started to play
some couples choose to "make an entrance" — especially when
the dress is formal ... the staircase is curved — it reminds me
of the grand finale at the pantomime. (*He smiles*) Certainly
some of the gowns have a feeling for "the theatrical" — or
am I getting too conventional in my old age? And come to
think of it, "gown" is a word my mother would have used ...
the "living language changeth."

Pause

Old ... I find it difficult to articulate "old" — whether as a noun or an adjective — it takes me by surprise — the "being old" — yet I am. Seventy years — old. (*He drinks*) They both seemed quite charming and pleased to talk ... the two women I met ... on my walk — very friendly. And I'm tired of my own company. (*Beat*) The question is, after dinner, do I issue an invitation? And to them both? Yes ... yes of course to them both. Just for drinks ... here on the deck. I've been on my own for too long ... far too long. (*He finishes the gin and tonic*) So Stephen, fortified with the G and T — nothing ventured? Be brave ... why not?

The Lights fade to black-out

Waiters enter to swiftly strike and reset properties for Scene 2

Scene 2

After dinner

When the Lights come up there is strong moonlight which illuminates the scene as well as the battery-operated, small candles on the tables

Stephen is standing DL *looking out to sea. In a moment Isabel makes an entrance — resplendent in her lavender three-quarter-length dress and holding an evening handbag. She wears a pearl necklace and matching earrings*

Isabel I'm sorry I'm late. I had to go back to the dining-room. (*She indicates*) Left my handbag.
Stephen And you found it — good. (*Beat*) I hope you don't mind being invited to come out here ... for a nightcap?
Isabel Not at all, it's such a lovely evening.
Stephen This is a sheltered corner — where one can sit and have a quiet drink. (*He politely moves a chair at the upstage table indicating for Isabel to sit*)

Isabel does so

I discovered it last night. And you discovered it this afternoon.

We hear distant applause followed by "Hello Young Lovers"

Isabel I discovered it on the first day — and our cabin is quite near.

Stephen Did I say quiet?

Isabel It's the resident pianist — "An Hour with Rodgers and Hammerstein" — it was in the ship's bulletin. (*She listens and recognizes* "Hello Young Lovers") Yes ... *The King and I* ... I saw the revival at the London Palladium.

Stephen Recently?

Isabel Oh no — quite some years ago.

Stephen (*after a beat*) Is your friend going to join us?

Isabel Friend? Oh, Margot. She's gone to get my stole. She's my daughter.

Stephen I hadn't realized.

Isabel (*delighted, as if it were a compliment*) You flatter me ... but thank you. (*Beat*) She won't be long. She knows where to come.

Stephen What I meant is ... she ...

Isabel waits for a second compliment

... she doesn't have your features.

Isabel No. No, she takes after her father, in temperament also. (*Beat*) My husband died many years ago.

Stephen I'm sorry.

Isabel It was a long illness. In the end — a relief — for us both.

Stephen I understand.

Isabel (*tentatively*) You also?

Stephen Yes. My wife died a year ago.

Isabel (*after a beat*) A difficult time. My daughter lives quite close to me so I can call on her — when I need help, when

I'm lonely — that's if she can fit me into her busy schedule. (*Critically*) Children! (*After a beat*) Have you any?
Stephen No. We had hoped, but ... it didn't happen.
Isabel I'm sorry.

Beat, then Stephen looks in the direction of the off stage bar

Stephen No waiter — but they do serve drinks out here.
Isabel From my experience at tea I think you might have to go to the bar.
Stephen What would you like?
Isabel Cointreau would be perfect.
Stephen And your daughter?
Isabel (*critically*) Amaretto with ice.
Stephen Won't be a moment. (*He smiles*) I hope. Excuse me.

Stephen exits to the off stage bar

Isabel rises and moves towards the DL *rail listening to the pianist who is playing* "Some Enchanted Evening"

In a moment Margot enters wearing a simple but attractive evening dress and an evening jacket. She is not wearing her spectacles and has put on a little make-up. She carries Isabel's matching lavender stole and crosses to her

Margot Mother. You had better put it on — it's cooler than I thought. (*She passes her the stole*)
Isabel Thank you, dear.
Margot All on your own? Has he abandoned you?
Isabel He's gone to get the drinks.
Margot How are you getting on?
Isabel Extremely well. (*She looks in the direction of the bar. Confidentially*) I've already learned quite a lot about him — tell you later. He's rather shy — but I like that — not at all pushy — very courteous.

Margot Mother ... don't get carried away.
Isabel I'm not — I'm just enjoying a little ... attention.

Stephen enters

Stephen The drinks are on their way.
Isabel Lovely! It's ridiculous, but we haven't got round to
introductions — have we? I'm Isabel Anderson and I told you
that this is my daughter — Margot. (*She laughs*) Shall we be
formal? (*She holds out her hand*)
Stephen Why not?

He shakes Isabel's and Margot's hands

Very pleased to meet you ... both of you.

Margot and Isabel look at him

Yes, and then there's me! I'm Stephen, Stephen Brown. (*Beat*)
Well ... introductions over ... shall we sit down?
Isabel And wait for the drinks.
Stephen Exactly.

*Stephen indicates a chair for Margot to sit at the upstage table
and Isabel returns to her chair while he moves an upright chair
from the upstage rail and places it between the two women*

(*Taking out a cheroot and a lighter*) Do you mind?
Isabel Not at all.

Stephen lights his cheroot

Is this your first cruise?
Stephen Er ... yes.
Margot And no doubt you won't want to go on another.
Isabel Margot!

Stephen (*enjoying Margot's frankness*) Possibly. I love the excursions, full of interest ... but the days at sea are too highly organized ... with some rather lacklustre talks. (*He smiles*) And the late-night theatre revue is not really to my taste.

Margot And one can get tired of the view — seascapes can be unbelievably tedious.

Stephen (*smiling*) Yes ... my walk seemed to take forever, but I went back to my cabin and got my walkman ——

Margot (*amazed*) Walkman?

Stephen (*amused*) Yes ... I'm a bit of a technophobe — must move with the times. But it helped — the music, I mean. (*He rises and crosses to the downstage table for the ashtray*)

Isabel What music?

Stephen Mozart — my favourite.

Margot Opera?

Stephen No — the piano concertos.

Isabel Do you play ... the piano?

Stephen A little — but only for myself. (*He smiles*) I don't inflict it on other people.

Margot And your walk — did you complete the mile?

Stephen Two actually. (*He returns to the table and sits*)

Margot Well done ——

Isabel (*interrupting*) I know what you mean — about the days at sea — but I love it when we sail into each port — then the view is fascinating — all those little islands ...

The Waiter enters carrying a tray with their drinks — for evening duty he wears a colourful waistcoat with a small gold badge which states his name

Waiter Here we are. Let me guess. (*He serves the drinks with a certain flourish*) The Cointreau for *signora*, brandy for *signore*, and of course ... amaretto with ice for the *signorina* ... cin cin!

Margot *Cin cin!* (*She raises her glass*)

The others follow her lead

Stephen ⎫ (*together*) *Cin cin*!
Isabel ⎭

Waiter *Signore*. (*He passes the bill and biro to Stephen*)

Stephen signs it and then the Waiter gives him a copy

Stephen (*returning the biro*) Thank you.

Waiter (*to Margot*) Did the *signorina* enjoy her swim?

Margot Very much, thank you.

Waiter But not like the Mediterranean.

Margot No ... but quiet ... tranquil.

Waiter Ah yes — *tranquillo* ... you are a good swimmer?

Isabel (*frostily*) Thank you. That will be all.

The Waiter exits

Margot (*reproving*) Mother.

Isabel I'm sorry but he's just a little too ... familiar.

Stephen (*to Isabel*) I don't think he meant to overstep the mark ... but ... (*to Margot*) ... it would seem that you have an admirer.

Margot All the waiters flirt with the women — haven't you noticed? It's part of the job and especially if one's obviously not with a partner. (*Imitating*) "*Signorina*" — at my age! Shades of *The Roman Spring of Mrs Stone*.

Stephen Mrs Stone?

Margot (*enjoying dramatizing*) A well-heeled woman — of a certain age, alone in Rome — living with her gigolo.

Stephen (*to Isabel*) I'm lost.

Margot Tennessee Williams — a short story.

Stephen I don't know it — but I know some of his plays.

Margot (*surprised*) You go to the theatre?

Stephen Yes, quite a lot.

Isabel (*at last able to interrupt*) Margot — sorry dear — perhaps I was overreacting ... (*to Stephen*) ... with the waiter. I had a rather difficult time earlier today. (*She smiles*) I mustn't hold it against him.

Stephen The staff work very long hours.

Tension between Margot and Isabel shows in the following brief exchange

Margot And I wonder what the rate of pay is. Just hope they are not being taken advantage of.

Isabel Well, with the recession I suppose some of them are only too pleased to have a job.

Margot That's not the point, Mother. I wonder if they even get the minimum wage?

Isabel Well they do have the tips — and that will add up considerably.

Margot And that's not the answer. It's like being dependent on charity — and some people can be incredibly mean.

Isabel (*controlled but annoyed*) I hope you are not suggesting —— ?

Margot Of course not. (*To Stephen*) Sorry ... but it just seemed a significant issue ... worth discussing. (*She finishes her drink*) Maybe I'm tired — and not in the mood for ——

Stephen Small talk?

Margot (*smiling*) Yes. (*Beat. She rises. To Stephen*) If you'll excuse me I think I'll have a stroll and retire.

Stephen rises

Thanks for the drink — very nice of you to invite us. Really.

Stephen My pleasure.

Margot Perhaps I'll see you in the Hermitage?

Stephen I hope so. Good-night.

Margot Good-night.

Isabel (*firmly*) Don't go for a stroll — not at this time.

Margot I'll see how I feel, Mother. (*Enjoying*) Might go to the casino and gamble my life's savings — you never can tell.

Margot exits

Isabel I'm sorry. Margot was always somewhat ... er ... high-spirited.

Stephen (*sitting on Margot's empty chair*) No need to apologize .... she's obviously a young woman with a mind of her own.

Isabel However in company her forthright attitude can seem somewhat out of place.

Stephen Not at all — what she had to say was quite refreshing. Is she married?

Isabel Unfortunately no. We tried with friends from the Rotary Club but all to no avail. She doesn't seem to have success with men. She did have a long-standing admirer — very secretive about him — but for some reason it fizzled out. She's getting on — I keep telling her — she's well over forty.

Stephen To me forty is still young — very young!

Isabel She spends far too much time at school — a private girls' school — very little time for me.

Stephen And her subject?

Isabel English ... she even directs the school play, mostly Shakespeare. (*She smiles*) Not exactly my cup of tea. Last year she did *The Importance of Being Earnest* — but the girls weren't really up to it.

Stephen Still, very adventurous. I admire that.

Isabel Oh yes ... so do I.

Stephen stubs out his cheroot

Stephen (*being polite*) Now tell me about you?

Isabel (*flattered, rising*) There's nothing much to tell.

Stephen Come, come. I'm sure there is.

Isabel I look after my flat — in Streatham — near the common. I enjoy gardening ... I'm quite a good cook. And I love sewing — mainly embroidery and quilting. (*She paces to* UC *of table*) What else do I do? Actually I help quite a lot in running a charity shop for the Macmillan Nurses — I was a nurse before I married.

Stephen So ... you have a full life. That's good.

Isabel And you? What did you do before you before you ——

Stephen Retired?

Isabel (*sitting on the centre chair next to Stephen*) I hesitated because ——

Stephen Because you were being polite. I retired, oh, five years ago ... from the Civil Service. I used to work at the Treasury.

Isabel How impressive.

Stephen Not really ... but often demanding ... meeting deadlines ... especially when the budget was approaching.

Isabel The "red box".

Stephen Yes. (*He smiles*) Many a Chancellor has passed me by ... so to speak.

Isabel Fascinating.

Stephen Not really — at the end of the day ... it was just a job.

Waiter enters with his tray

Waiter *Signore* — can I get you another drink? This bar close early tonight. Drinking goes on in upstairs bar.

Stephen (*to Isabel*) Would you like another Cointreau?

Isabel No thanks.

Stephen (*to the Waiter*) Thank you, but we won't have another drink. Good-night.

Waiter *Buona notte, signore* ... and *signora*. (*He clears the glasses*) Listen — they play the waltz — above in Rendezvous Room. (*He smiles*) I know the repertoire — the last waltz.

Waiter exits

Isabel (*listening to "Out of My Dreams"*) One of my favourites. (*She sways to the music and looks at Stephen*) The waltz from *Oklahoma*. (*Beat*) So ... shall we ... waltz?

Stephen I'm not very good.

Isabel We'll manage. Give it a try.

Stephen (*after a beat, then smiling*) May I have the pleasure?

Isabel I haven't heard those words in a very long time.

Stephen I don't think they are used any more.

Isabel I would be delighted.

They dance — Stephen is rather self-conscious while Isabel is much more relaxed

Stephen You see ... I'm no Fred Astaire.

Isabel You are doing very nicely.

Stephen (*laughing*) Damning with faint praise.

Isabel Not at all. You have an excellent sense of rhythm. Try the reverse turn ...

Stephen (*attempting to do the reverse turn*) Sorry ... (*He stops dancing*)

Isabel That wasn't at all bad. You just need a little more tuition. (*She smiles enigmatically*) Give it time.

Stephen I can't remember when I last danced.

Isabel Maybe you shouldn't let it be so long.

Stephen Maybe. (*Beat, then he looks at his watch*) Well I suppose it is time to ...

Isabel ... call it a day?

Stephen It's an early start tomorrow — St Petersburg.

Isabel Yes ... but let me persuade you to dance until the end? (*She smiles*) Until the end of "the last waltz". (*Beat*) Please?

Stephen (*smiling*) How can I refuse?

They start to dance and then the Lights fade to black-out

In the black-out Margot, Isabel and Stephen go to their positions as detailed in the next scene

SCENE 3

Two days later — before and after dinner

Margot is seen in isolated light at the DR rail and is wearing a simple, silk summer dress and smart shoes

Margot I've had a great time — *two* days with excursions. First it was the Hermitage — but they just didn't give us enough

time. Stephen and I slipped away from the group and went up
to the top gallery — saw a Matisse that one could die for ...
Mother couldn't face the climb. And she wasn't feeling well
again today in Helsinki — didn't go to the cathedral — had to
sit quietly in the shade — so Stephen came with me. He's well
informed — full of surprises. He went to Oxford — degree in
English and then went on to London — School of Economics.
But the surprises weren't all "academic" — that is ... when we
were on our own ... briefly holding my arm on the stairs — as
if I needed assistance, making eye contact just that half second
longer than one expects ... and (*smiling*) savouring my "witti-
cisms" with just a little more relish than they deserve. (*Beat*)
Oh dear Mama — you're not going to take very kindly to these
attentions — are you?

*The light cross fades to Isabel who is seen in isolated light
standing UC, wearing a long dressing gown. She is holding a
small compact and looking at her face in the mirror*

Isabel I'm not doing my make-up again — just don't feel up to
it. (*Beat*) Come to think of it, I wasn't very well yesterday — a
long day. After the Hermitage it was the Great Palace — lots
of slow walking — that's what finishes me off. (*Beat*) I must
say Stephen's very energetic for his age ... managed to keep
up with Margot's pace — seems to get on with her and (*know-
ingly*) I think that's a good thing. He has been so attentive ...
last night he invited us for drinks on the deck — and *again* for
tonight. (*She smiles*) From time to time he would catch my eye
and smile — you know how it is ... and today in Helsinki he
insisted that I rest while he and Margot went up to the cathedral.
Dear man — he found me a quiet café where I could rest. Yes,
Isabel ... I definitely think there is ... "interest". (*She looks at
herself in the the compact mirror. Reassured, she smiles and
uses the powder puff*)

*The light cross fades to Stephen at the DL rail. He is wearing
the same lightweight suit that we saw in* SCENE 2 — *but now*

he is wearing an open-necked shirt and holding a glass of orange juice

Isabel and Margot exit

Stephen (*drinking and then indicating the glass*) No gin — just orange juice. I want a clear head for this evening. (*Beat*) Margot's just phoned — her mother's not feeling well so she won't be joining us for drinks which is quite a relief ... it means that I can speak frankly ... put my cards on the table, so to speak. Tonight the dress code is again "smart-casual"... so I thought an open neck shirt — that's now the fashion, isn't it? Yes ... it would be too stuffy to wear a tie. (*Pause*) I'm excited ... and nervous — rather stupid at my age ... but she already makes me feel ... young. I haven't felt like this in such a long time ... (*He moves away from the rail*)

The general lighting comes in — moonlight as in SCENE 2

But ... I must tread carefully. Not easy. Not at all ... easy. (*He finishes the orange juice*)

The Waiter enters with a small battery-operated candle which he places at the downstage table

Stephen crosses to the upstage table with his empty glass

Waiter Good-evening, sir.
Stephen Good-evening.
Waiter Did you enjoy Helsinki?
Stephen Yes ... yes very much.
Waiter I hope to go ... maybe next trip I ask.
Stephen Yes ... yes you must — ask.
Waiter We get little free time.
Stephen I'm sorry.
Waiter *Cosa*?

Stephen That you get little free time.
Waiter *Si*.
Stephen What is your name?

Margot enters wearing the same dress as in SCENE 2 *but with an interesting evening jacket*

Waiter Mario — (*he shows his badge*) — my name.
Stephen (*looking*) Ah yes ... I need spectacles.
Margot So ... I'm not the only one — to need spectacles.
Stephen I'm glad that you could come.
Margot So am I.
Waiter (*moving the downstage table and the two chairs to a slightly more central position*) Would you like this table, sir? Different view?
Stephen Yes ... that will be fine.
Margot (*wandering over to the railing*) Different? The view is the same.
Stephen The same?
Margot (*gesturing out front*) The sea!
Stephen (*to Margot*) Then we shall have to imagine that it is different.
Waiter *Imaginare* ... yes and helped by the moon ...
Margot Yes. (*She looks up to the sky*) It is a "full moon".
Waiter *Luna piena*.
Margot (*savouring the pronunciation and looking at the moon*) "*Luna piena*."
Waiter (*smiling*) *Si*. (*Beat*) What would you like to drink, sir?
Stephen (*to Margot*) The same?
Margot Please.
Waiter Then amaretto with ice for Miss Anderson and ... a brandy for Mr Brown?
Stephen That's right. Thank you.

Stephen offers the Waiter his ship's plastic identity card which the Waiter refuses

Waiter (*pleased that he can impress*) It is all right — Mr Brown
— (*smiling*) Cabin B — seventy-three.

Stephen That is correct.

Waiter Back in a moment.

Waiter exits

Stephen It would seem that we are regulars.

Margot Well, we are — three nights running. (*Teasing*) People
are beginning to talk.

Stephen (*shocked*) Are they?

Margot (*laughing*) Of course not — joking. What is there to
talk about?

Stephen That depends ——

Margot On what?

Stephen On what you have to say ——

Margot About what?

Stephen About the last three days.

Margot What I have to say? You're talking in riddles.

Stephen Am I? (*He places his arm round her shoulder*) Come
and sit down. The drinks will be here ... and then, Margot, we
can talk. (*Beat*) Please.

Margot crosses to the table and sits

Incidentally — why were you called Margot?

Margot My grandmother loved the ballet.

Stephen Of course — Margot Fonteyn. (*He looks at her*) It
suits you.

Margot I can't think why. (*She smiles*) I was a great disappoint-
ment — I can't dance.

Stephen That's fortunate — neither can I.

The Waiter quickly enters with the drinks and serves them

Waiter Here we are ... quickly for you. Bingo upstairs — I may
have to help.

Margot (*to Stephen*) I thought bingo was only on the internet these days.

Stephen (*to Waiter*) In England the bingo halls close down ... they end ... *finito*.

Waiter (*enjoying his own joke*) So ... that is why people come on cruise.

Margot (*laughing*) Some of them, yes.

Waiter Please sign. (*He passes the bill and a biro*)

Stephen signs

Will that be all, Mr Brown? Miss Anderson?

Stephen Yes, thank you.

The Waiter exits

He's quite a congenial fellow.

Margot Well ... he certainly wants to make an impression.

Stephen picks up his drink

Stephen Cheers.

Margot (*chinking his glass*) Cheers.

They drink. Pause

Stephen Margot?

Margot Yes?

Stephen I promised myself that I would come straight to the point — and not procrastinate.

Margot Procrastinate?

Stephen Giving myself time to think.

Margot About what?

Stephen Margot — I've enjoyed the excursions — that is, being with you. (*Beat*) I have, er ... deliberately sought your company ...

Margot (*joking*) You mustn't make it sound like the confessional.

Stephen Please. I have tried, I hope, to make you know that I ... that I care about you.

Margot Yes, I have been aware. (*Beat*) Stephen — it's a lovely compliment — don't think that I don't enjoy being with you. I do. You're full of surprises and you make me feel ... important — and that's lovely.

Stephen Well, that's a splendid start.

Stephen leaves his drink on the table and rises, crossing to centre downstage

Come and look at the sea

Margot I can see it from here.

Stephen *Please*.

Margot joins him

(*Looking out to sea*) "The moon shines bright. (*Beat*) In such a night as this ..."

Margot "When the sweet wind did gently kiss the trees ..."

Stephen "And they did make no noise."

Margot You rehearsed it.

Stephen I'm afraid I did.

Margot Well — it was charming.

Stephen I once played Lorenzo.

Margot When?

Stephen University — I keep it a dark secret — Drama Soc.

Margot O.U.D.S?

Stephen nods

Another surprise.

Stephen Lorenzo ... is my "prelude"... it brings me to ... maybe the biggest surprise. (*Beat*) Margot, would you consider marrying me?

Margot Marrying you? (*Shocked and amazed — she almost starts to laugh*)

Stephen You find it funny?

Margot No — not you ... please, not you. I was thinking of Mother — she thinks that you're interested in her!

Stephen That's ridiculous. I never gave her any encouragement.

Margot She thinks you did. (*Teasing*) Looking after her on the excursions — finding places where she could rest — getting her cups of tea ...

Stephen That was only so that I could be with you.

Margot Well, to be honest, I wasn't sure. Stephen — I'm teasing. Mother lets her imagination run away. I wanted to warn you, but at the same time I didn't want to spoil her having a little fun. I should have known that it would "all end in tears" — well, I hope not literally.

Stephen Never mind your mother. I've just asked you to marry me.

Margot Sorry — but as the saying goes in romantic fiction — "it is very sudden". You hardly know me.

Stephen I think I know you well enough ... otherwise I wouldn't have made my proposal.

Margot I wouldn't have thought of you as an impetuous man.

Stephen I'm not. (*Beat*) But since St Petersburg I've been able to think of little else — except you.

Margot I'm ... I'm a little bit overwhelmed.

Stephen Don't be. It can all be on your terms — the Hampstead flat is quite large — I think you would like it. You can go on teaching if you want to ... and directing the plays ...

Margot Stop ... not so fast ... not so fast.

Stephen Sorry. (*Beat*) Of course there is the difference in age — a sensitive issue — about which only you can decide. I don't want you to think that I'm looking for someone to take care of me if I'm ill.

Margot (*smiling*) No doubt you're in BUPA.

Stephen (*enjoying her retort*) As a matter of fact I am. But seriously, I'm in good health and hope to be for a good many years. Nevertheless I looked very closely at myself in the mirror this morning and I know I'm showing my age ... that, perhaps for you, could be a very big turn off.

Margot Not at all — you're an attractive man.

Stephen Come, come ...

Margot Well OK ... "distinguished."

Stephen Methinks the lady doth protest ...

Margot She's trying not to. (*Beat*) Stephen — I'm touched ... and flattered. Thank you. (*Beat*) But I'm not in love with you.

Stephen I realize that — but perhaps that would grow — the love — being together?

Margot (*warmly*) Oh, Stephen — what can I say?

Silence. They both look out to sea

I loved the excerpt from *The Merchant*.

Stephen (*looking at her*) I can go on ... (*taking her hand*) "In such a night did young Lorenzo swear he loved her well." (*He kisses her hand*)

Margot "Methinks too well". (*She releases her hand. Pause*) Good-night Stephen.

Stephen Good-night ... and think about what I have said.

Margot Yes ... I will.

Stephen And your mother?

Margot I think you had better leave Mother to me.

Stephen Yes ... thank you. (*Beat*) Stay a little longer. Have another drink?

Margot I don't think so. Not tonight. But Stockholm tomorrow.

Margot exits

Stephen (*calling out*)Yes. Stockholm.

The Waiter enters and collects the glasses from the downstage table

Stephen lights a cheroot by the DL rail

Waiter Another brandy, sir?
Stephen Yes.
Waiter (*looking round*) And the lady?
Stephen Nothing for the lady.
Waiter (*crossing to the upstage table and collecting Stephen's
    empty orange juice glass*) She has gone?
Stephen (*looking out to sea*) Yes. (*Beat*) She has gone.

*The Waiter looks at Stephen and senses his preoccupation
and exits*

*For a few seconds Stephen smokes looking out to the sea as the
Lights fade to black-out*

Scene 4

Two days later. Mid afternoon

*There is still a little warmth in the sun but the lighting at first
encloses Isabel on her upstage wooden armchair. She is reading
a book, wears an attractive summer dress and a cardigan and
her legs are covered by a rug. In a moment she looks up*

Isabel Unfortunately I didn't get to Stockholm. Very frustrat-
    ing. The Nurse prescribed some medication — tummy upset
    — I knew that seafood salad was a mistake ... so I felt I had
    to play safe ... and now I'm feeling much better and wished I
    had gone. I had a quiet morning and this afternoon came out
    here — got fed up of being in the cabin. (*Beat*) Margot will
    tell me all about it — what she and Stephen got up to. (*Beat*)
    It's going so quickly — only four days left — then it will be
    home ... all over. But we can exchange addresses — phone
    numbers — and Hampstead isn't very far away. So just relax,
    Isabel — relax and look forward to this evening.

The general lighting comes in

The Waiter enters with Isabel's tea

Waiter Here we are, Mrs Anderson — the camomile tea — for
the *paziente* — how do you say — the patient?
Isabel (*smiling*) I'm hardly a patient, but thank you. And thank
you for the rug.
Waiter My pleasure. Is cooler today. The sun not so strong.
Isobel No, but I prefer that. Yesterday it was too hot.
Waiter *Si*. And Mrs Anderson is feeling better?
Isabel (*pleased that he knows her name*) Yes, quite a lot better.
Waiter That is good.

*Pause. The Waiter passes Isabel a biro with the bill which
she signs. He pours out her tea. Isabel returns the bill and
the pen*

Thank you. (*He takes in the scene. Looking at his watch*)
Any moment ... and all the people will return from excursion.
Without them it is peaceful — time to ... what do you say ...
to draw the breath. We work hard, madam, late hours ... very
little free time.
Isabel Yes it must be a long day.
Waiter *Si* ... *very* long. But tonight I finish early which is good.
(*Confidentially*) It's karaoke night — very noisy — many
people in the bar.
Isabel Well ... enjoy your break.
Waiter I will. Will that be all, *signora*?
Isabel Yes, thank you.

*The Waiter starts to exit but Isabel takes a ten euro note from
her handbag*

(*Calling to him*) Mario ... just a moment.
Mario Si — *signora*?
Isabel (*holding up the ten euro note*) A little something, Mario
... for you.

Waiter (*taking the note*) Mrs Anderson is too kind. (*He kisses her hand*) Molte grazie — molte.

The Waiter starts to exit and turns

(*Calling*) Arrividerci, madam.
Isabel (*surprising herself and calling out*) Arrividerci!

The Waiter exits

After a moment Isabel picks up her book

Damn! I've lost my place.

Margot enters wearing slacks, sensible top and a cardigan tied round her waist. Over her shoulder is a camera and she carries a handbag. She is wearing her glasses

Margot There you are. I got back early ... went to the cabin — felt concerned.
Isabel No need to be — I'm much better. I'm relaxed. Had a little chat with our waiter — you know who I mean — Mario. When you get to know him he's really quite charming.
Margot You have changed your tune. (*She places the camera, handbag and cardigan on one of the café tables*)
Isabel I felt sorry for him. But never mind Mario — how was Stockholm? (*Beat*) Is Stephen with you?
Margot No ... he went to reception to get some money.
Isabel Did he send any message — ask after me?
Margot (*after a pause*) Mother — this will come as ... well, yes ... as a "surprise", but I'm not prepared to put it off — otherwise this evening would be a farce.
Isabel This evening? What are you on about?
Margot If this were the police they would begin by saying — "I'm afraid I have some bad news."
Isabel (*rising*) Is it Stephen? Has there been an accident?
Margot Good heavens, no.

Relieved, Isabel sits

> There's no easy way round this. (*A beat. She sits at the table facing Isabel*) Stephen has asked me to marry him.

Isabel (*after a beat*) *You!*

Margot Yes, Mother, me.

Isabel (*after a beat*) I don't believe it!

The following exchange slowly gathers its resentful momentum from both sides — it is taut and well paced

Margot Am I so unattractive? Is it so unthinkable that a man should propose to me? That a man should desire me?

Isabel Perhaps he thinks of you as an insurance policy for his old age.

Margot I will ignore that remark. I don't think that age comes into the equation. It didn't put you off.

Isabel Because we were more or less the same age. He must be thirty years older than you — at least. What is the man thinking of?

Margot Maybe sex, Mother.

Isabel Margot — don't be disgusting. And how long has this been going on? ... Behind my back — my own daughter.

Margot Oh don't sound so melodramatic. We only met him a few days ago.

Isabel Exactly — but you didn't waste any time, did you?

Margot Mother, you have got this out of all proportion. I didn't encourage him ... It was just that the more we talked, the more we seemed to get on — enjoying each other's company. As far as I was concerned that was as far as it went — hence his proposal was quite unexpected.

Isabel (*cynically*) Really?

Margot Mother, you made your bid and he didn't respond. You went on clutching at straws — romanticizing — as is your way. Be honest — he didn't really encourage you.

Isabel I'm not a fool. There were signs — signals — I know about these things.

Margot You misinterpreted them and when he did make a fuss of you, it was because he wanted some time with me. He didn't want "Mother to come too".

Isabel You can be very cruel, Margot. (*Beat*) Well? Are you going to ...?

Margot looks at her

Marry him?

Margot He only proposed last night. I said that I would ... think about it.

Isabel Playing hard to get? He might change his mind.

Margot From what he said — I don't think he will.

Isabel (*after a beat*) This all puts me in a very difficult position. Embarrassing ... humiliating. I shall have dinner in my cabin. In no way am I going into the dining-room tonight.

Margot And what about tomorrow's excursion — Oslo?

Isabel Oh never fear — if I go — I shall go on my own.

Margot It's up to you. Stephen would be his usual friendly self.

Isabel (*in a formidable tone*) I had rather keep my distance from Stephen ... that is until I have reviewed the situation. And then ... I shall speak to him.

Margot You sound like Lady Bracknell.

Isabel (*strongly*) Don't be flippant. Someone has to look after your interests.

Margot (*her speech growing in emotional intensity — as if she has suddenly found her own voice*) Listen, Mother — and listen carefully. My life is my concern — not yours. I will make my own decisions. Ever since Dad died I have allowed myself to be at your beck and call. But I'm forty-four years old and it's not too late to change my life, perhaps to get away, to have *adventure,* to surprise myself and *if* that "adventure" is to be with Stephen, then so be it. (*Beat*) But I will make up my own mind, in my own time, without any interference from you. Is that quite clear, Mother?

Isabel I had no idea that you harboured such ... resentment. (*She picks up her book*) I have a splitting headache which is hardly surprising. And now — I want to be on my own — but then it would seem that I have been on my own for a very long time.

Isabel exits with as much dignity as she can muster

Margot feels cold and puts on her cardigan and paces downstage

The Waiter enters with a tray to collect Isabel's tea things

Waiter (*seeing Margot*) Your mother? She is OK?
Margot She's gone to her cabin — she's tired. (*She looks up to the sky and takes comfort from her cardigan*)
Margot I think it is going to rain.
Waiter Yes ... I must put away the rug ... the cushions.

He doesn't move — their eyes meet

Margot Which part of Italy do you come from?
Waiter From Napoli — Naples.
Margot How lovely. I must go there one day. People used to say "see Naples and die".
Waiter Yes, is true — *bella città* ... beautiful city. If you visit when I am home — I show you everything.
Margot Thank you.
Waiter You would come to Napoli?
Margot (*smiling*) Perhaps.
Waiter To please me?
Margot (*after a beat*) Perhaps.
Waiter Miss Anderson is ... how you say ... teasing me.
Margot No, I'm not. Just that ... the opportunity to come to Naples, it has been ... difficult for me.
Waiter Well — you must find the way ... to visit.
Margot Perhaps — one day. Who knows?
Waiter (*taking a pace towards her*) And I take you to Sorrento — *molto romantico*.
Margot Please — can I have a brandy?
Waiter Of course. (*Surprised*) Brandy?

Margot Yes ... I need one, something strong.
Waiter A double?

Margot nods

> Si — and *I* will get one for Miss Margot. *Offro io* — how do
> you say? ... My treat.

Margot No ... I couldn't possibly allow you ...
Waiter *Please* — (*standing very close to her*) — it would be
my pleasure.
Margot (*not withdrawing*) Mario ... I ...
Waiter The first time you say my name. (*Lightly touching her
cheek*) Your beautiful eyes ...
Margot You flatter me ...

She doesn't move and this gives him confidence

Waiter (*wooing her*) No ... the first time I see you I remember
your eyes. (*Beat*) Tonight ... tonight I finish at nine — my
friend's cabin is free — it is *libera* — private ... if you would
like we meet and ... (*He moves as if to kiss her*)
Margot (*standing back a pace*) Like? *No* — I would not like.
(*Turning away from him*) *Please* ... please forgive me.
Waiter (*embarrassed*) No ... no, my mistake ... *Mi dispiace
molto* ... *very* sorry. (*Beat*) Will that be all?
Margot *Yes*.
Waiter The brandy?
Margot Forget the brandy ... (*Beat — then firmly*) That will be all.

> *The Waiter is glad of an excuse to leave and quickly picks up
> the tray with the tea things and exits*

> (*Strongly to herself*) You fool ... you stupid fool.

*She moves to the DL rail area and the Lights close in around
her*

Did *I* initiate that "encounter"? I don't know — I must have. The point is ... I would ... "have liked"... for that second I have to admit it. He's handsome, young, sexy. *Yes* ... I liked the idea. Of what? Casual sex. Not even a one night stand — probably half an hour in a sweaty subterranean cabin. Is that all that's left? Relying on the kindness of strangers. (*Beat*) Most of the men of my age are married — they're only interested in "a bit on the side". When promises are made, from my limited experience, they're not kept ... hence he left me — high and dry ... (*Visibly moved*) ... after *all* those years. (*Beat*) As for divorced men — they're looking for a younger model than me. (*Beat*) Oh Stephen — I'm not going to settle for half.

The Lights fade to black-out

Scene 5

Two days later, early evening

There has been some rain and dark clouds still hover. The furniture remains the same as at the end of Scene 4 *but as it has been raining the chairs are leaning against the tables and the high armchair with cushions and rug has been struck*

Stephen is seen in enclosed light by the DR *rail. He is wearing a mackintosh and holding a letter*

Stephen Margot and her mother didn't show up for dinner again so I thought it best to keep a low profile. In any case I want Margot to have time to think — don't want her to feel under any ... pressure. (*Beat*) She didn't go on the main Oslo excursion but I saw her, near the royal palace ... getting into a taxi, on her own ... she didn't see me. Anyway she must have got back before me — as this was waiting. (*He glances at the letter*) She's sorry about last night — not meeting me — she says she was "under stress". Of course ... I can understand that.

(*Beat*) Anyway she wants to meet me ... here. (*He looks at his watch and moves in to a central area*)

The general lighting comes in

Any moment now. Somewhat ominous? I hope not. (*Beat*) Just to see her ... you know ... makes me feel good.

Stephen moves towards the UR *entrance*

Margot takes him by surprise and enters from the DL *entrance — she is wearing a raincoat and sensible shoes*

Margot (*after a beat*) Hello.

Stephen quickly turns to face her

I'm early.
Stephen Are you? (*Beat*) You have been missed.
Margot Have I? Well that's comforting.
Stephen (*after a beat*) If you want a coffee or anything we'll have to go indoors, but we won't have our waiter — he's been moved to the Crow's Nest ... you know, the bar on the top deck. I bumped into him when I returned.
Margot The Italian?
Stephen Yes — Mario.
Margot Of course. (*Beat*) Did he say why? ... Why he was moving?
Stephen No — it was as if he was trying to avoid me. You know how normally he's so ebullient, so charming.
Margot Perhaps he was in a bad mood — perhaps he had come across some resistance.
Stephen Resistance?
Margot To his charm.
Stephen Perhaps. (*After a pause*) Well ... would you like to go in and have a coffee?
Margot No thanks — I've just had a snack. And you?

Stephen No, I'm fine.

Margot (*after a beat*) So, you went to Oslo?

Stephen Yes — the official tour of the city, a long day — but I enjoyed it. And your mother?

Margot She decided not to come — because of the weather — well that was the excuse. So I ... I went to Ibsen's apartment.

Stephen I wish I had known. Is that where he wrote?

Margot Yes, well, for the last twelve years of his life.

Stephen What was it like?

Margot Like ... walking on to a set for *A Doll's House*.

Stephen Where Nora was "liberated" ... from husband and children?

Margot Yes. Brave Nora. (*Beat*) I didn't stay long — I don't think I was in the mood.

Pause

Stephen You said in your letter that you were "under stress"? Your mother?

Margot Oh ... everything. My mother ... myself... and you.

Stephen Your *mother* first. Did she give you a hard time?

Margot To be expected. Antlers locked. She enjoys the high drama. Impossible woman, infuriating. Of course — given time she'll get over it — she always does.

Stephen Larkin was right.

Margot looks at him

About our parents, they ——

Margot They fuck us up.

Stephen (*smiling*) Quite. (*Beat*) And what about *you?*

Margot It's nothing really — I just made a stupid mistake.

Stephen We can all make ... "mistakes".

Margot (*beat*) I will tell you ... I will, Stephen ... but not just now.

Stephen Then you can tell me when you're ready — or ... not at all ... whatever. (*Beat*) So ... Let's return again *to me*. What stress am *I* causing? Other than wanting you to make up your mind. Is it the difference in our age?

Margot I told you ——

Stephen Yes, you did — but there are things perhaps you haven't considered. Your friends? You have to accept that some of them will be very critical — even censorious.

Margot Then they wouldn't be my friends any longer. (*Beat*) Stephen — I need to ask you this. (*Beat*) Are you in love with me?

Stephen Let me answer your question — with my question. "Love" — *what is it?*

Margot ... I'm waiting.

Stephen I'll do my best. (*Beat*) Love isn't ruled entirely by desire — which in any case may not be reciprocated.

Margot Oh yes, I know all about that. (*Beat*) But what about good old-fashioned "romance"?

Stephen Unfortunately it can quickly fade.

Margot Become ... an illusion?

Stephen Yes.

Margot What else?

Stephen There must be trust, and the "loved one" must be free. So Margot ... trust me.

Margot (*after a beat*) You said — "the loved one can be free"?

Stephen I did.

Margot Suddenly you make it so simple!

Stephen Simple?

Margot *Yes* ... why didn't I think of it before? And now it's *your* decision, not mine.

Stephen My decision?

Margot Yes. (*After a beat*) Don't propose marriage, Stephen — propose that I live with you.

Stephen *Live* with you?

Margot Don't sound shocked. Feel liberated.

Stephen I'm not shocked — just, er ... somewhat surprised ...

Margot Don't be — it is the twenty-first century ... don't get left behind. (*She takes his hand. With resolution*) And Stephen — I do trust you.

Stephen Then I won't get left behind.
Margot "What's to come is still *unsure*"?
Stephen Yes — "unsure"— but it's a risk worth taking. (*He gently kisses her*)
Margot That was rather nice.
Stephen For me too.

Beat. He holds her and they kiss more passionately

Margot Two more days ...
Stephen Yes. Then home. (*Beat*) Hampstead.
Margot (*smiling*) Yes ... Hampstead.
Stephen Let's celebrate. Champagne I think.

We hear the ship's siren — three times. Stephen takes out his cheroots and to his surprise Margot takes one which he lights

Voyager we set sail.
Margot Our adventure is about to begin.
Stephen Haven't you noticed? It has already begun. (*Beat*) And now for the champagne.

Margot links his arm and we hear a vibrant section of Mozart's Piano Concerto No. 23 as they joyfully cross upstage where we see them until they are virtually off stage — and so the Lights fade to black-out

FURNITURE AND PROPERTY LIST

On stage: White ship's railings
Two wooden, latticed chairs
Wooden, high-backed chair
Two low, latticed coffee tables. *On one*: handbag
           containing sun cream and sewing bag
Three matching chairs without arms
Section of two matching rail units
Matching wooden latticed table
Embroidery (for **Isabel**)
Travel book (for **Margot**)

Off stage: Tray. *On it*: teapot, milk, sugar and two cups (**Waiter**)
Tray. *On it*: small plate of postage-stamp sandwiches,
           small plate, napkin (**Waiter**)
Gin and tonic (**Stephen**)

Scene 2

Strike: Tea cups, milk and sugar, plates, napkin

Set: Small, battery-operated candles on tables

Off stage: Bill, biro, tray. *On it*: glasses of Cointreau, brandy,
           amaretto (**Waiter**)

Personal: **Isabel**: evening handbag
Stephen: cheroot, lighter

Scene 3

On stage: As before

Off stage: Glass of orange juice (**Stephen**)
               Small battery-operated candle (**Waiter**)
               Drinks, bill, biro (**Waiter**)

Personal: **Isabel**: compact mirror
               Stephen: cheroot, lighter

Scene 4

Set: Book, handbag containing ten euro note

Off stage: Tea things, bill, biro (**Waiter**)
               Camera, handbag (**Margot**)
               Tray (**Waiter**)

Personal: **Waiter**: watch

Scene 5

Strike: High-backed chair, cushions, rug

Set: Move chairs to lean against tables
               Letter (for **Stephen**)

Personal: **Stephen**: watch, cheroots, lighter

LIGHTING PLOT

Practical fittings required: battery-operated candles

Scene 1

To open: General exterior lighting, sunny

Cue 1	**Margot** paces over to ship's rail DL *Close Lights to* **Margot** DL	(Page 2)
Cue 2	**Isabel**: "Margot!" (first time) *Bring up Lights to full coverage*	(Page 2)
Cue 3	**Margot** sits and reads her travel book *Lighting loses its warmth*	(Page 3)
Cue 3	**Isabel**: "... with my pearls." *Fade Lights to black-out*	(Page 9)
Cue 4	**Margot** enters and moves to the rail DR *Bring up light on* **Margot** DR	(Page 10)
Cue 5	**Stephen** enters and moves to the rail DL *Cross fade to* **Stephen** DL	(Page 10)
Cue 6	**Stephen**: "Be brave ... why not?" *Fade Lights to black-out*	(Page 11)

Scene 2

To open: Night, strong moonlight

Cue 7   **Isabel** and **Stephen** start to dance   (Page 20)
            Fade Lights to black-out

SCENE 3

To open: Light on **Margot** DR

Cue 8   **Margot**: "... these attentions — are you?"   (Page 21)
            *Cross fade to **Isabel** UC*

Cue 9   **Isabel** uses the powder puff   (Page 22)
            *Cross fade to **Stephen** DL*

Cue 10   **Stephen** moves away from the rail   (Page 22)
            Bring up general lighting for a moonlit night,
            as SCENE 2

Cue 11   **Stephen** smokes for a few seconds   (Page 29)
            Fade Lights to black-out

SCENE 4

To open: Light UC on Isabel

Cue 12   "— relax and look forward to this evening."   (Page 30)
            Bring up general exterior lighting

Cue 13   **Margot** moves to DL rail area   (Page 36)
            *Lights close in on **Margot** DL*

Cue 14   **Margot**: "— I'm not going to settle for half."   (Page 37)
            Fade to black-out

SCENE 5

To open: Light DR on **Stephen**

Cue 15   **Stephen** moves to C   (Page 37)
            Bring up general exterior lighting, early evening,
            overcast

Cue 16   **Stephen** and **Margot** cross upstage   (Page 41)
            Fade Lights to black-out

EFFECTS PLOT

Cue 1   To open   (Page 1)
Vibrant short sequence from Mozart's "Piano Concerto No. 23", also used at the end of the play

Cue 2   **Stephen**: "And you discovered it this afternoon." (Page 12)
Distant applause followed by piano music: "Hello Young Lovers"

Cue 3   **Stephen** exits   (Page 13)
Piano music: "Some Enchanted Evening"

Cue 4   **Waiter** goes to exit   (Page 19)
Piano music: "Out of My Dreams"

Cue 5   **Stephen**: "Champagne I think."   (Page 41)
Ship's siren sounds four times

Cue 6   **Margot** links arms with **Stephen**   (Page 41)
Vibrant section of Mozart's "Piano Concerto No. 23"

Printed by The Kingfisher Press, London NW10 7AS